THE ENTROPY OF BIPOLAR DISORDER

A COLLECTION OF JOURNAL ENTRIES RELATED TO MENTAL ILLNESS AND BIPOLAR DISORDER

WORKINGS OF A BIPOLAR MIND
BOOK 4

JOHN MEDL

Formatted by Craig A. Price Jr.

ABOUT THE ENTROPY OF BIPOLAR DISORDER

This is the fourth book in a series of books written by John Medl. John takes us on another journey describing his daily struggles with bipolar disorder. His story is truly amazing. 14 years after being first hospitalized for a break in reality, he is now an author and mental health advocate. He discusses how he tries to help others and how it makes him feel better about his own situation. This book is full of raw emotions and feelings; the reader can actually feel the ups and downs of a bipolar man. Mental health professionals and students would also benefit from reading John's amazing story.

Tom

John keeps it real. If someone you know is dealing with mental health struggles this book can provide some suggestions that they too can get through the journey and enter a new way of life. He is able to provide first-hand experience and I fully support promoting the message.

Grant Williams

Mr. Medl, you are an inspiration! I hope you always know that. Your honesty and openness make people feel less alone. You bring hope to others. And as you know, that is a very precious gift. Thank you for sharing your life with us all.

Shana Koehler

John's books are a must have for anyone with, or anyone who loves, someone suffering from bipolar. It is a true insight of his day to day struggle. Very open and honest.

Susan Yacapraro

This book, in journal form, lays bare the daily struggles of a man with bipolar disorder. The story and the writing are true, unforgettable, and a lesson to be learned, for the writer is true and honest about his struggles and victories. A must for those wanting to know how mental illness is a stigma but also a proving ground for the soul, the mind. I very pleased to learn from this text. It helps me with my own journey and will help others. A must read book!

Albino Carrillo

CONTENTS

INTRODUCTION

This book is a collection of journal entries about my life and symptoms, along with letters to various people and organizations. Many of the journal entries are out of order, but I will do my best to explain each entry. My entire purpose of being an author and mental health advocate is to help people not feel so alone, and also to inspire others with my life story. Mental illness is a constant struggle, and often times, just getting through the day is a victory. I've tried to set the standards for my life at a higher level, but I am also struggling along with a lot of my readers, too. My writings are not just for the ill, but for their friends and family as well to help understand what someone who has a mental disorder may go through in a day, week, or years.

1 ENTRY 1

John Medl
Senior Reflection Paper
English 4 CP1

THE KEYSTONE READS 1959. I APPROACH THE LUMINOUS structure, my collared shirt and khaki shorts drenched in sweat on a hot late-August day. I am a freshman attending Archbishop Moeller High School for the first day in my high school career. The walls loom over my head as if to mock me, complemented by brass figurines perched on top of championship pedestals. All around are strange faces, except the dozen or so children that I had known since I was in first grade. I planned to sneak into Moeller without talking to too many people, get good grades, a diploma, go to college, and have Moeller not bat an eye at my existence. Familiarity and popularity were very familiar to me as a smaller child. I excelled in knothole sports (biggest kid on the team and probably the best). I've lived in the same house all my life in a small town, and I was somewhat of a troublemaker. All those combined with myself being a nice kid, funny for my age, and I could not walk two blocks in Deer Park without recognition. I wanted to stay away from that, not because I didn't like it, but simply because I knew the feeling. I wanted to be different at Moeller, just for the adventure and unpredictability of different. I would talk to my old friends who knew me already, stay in my corner of the school, and just get out. I realize how immature this train of thought was, but I believe I was very immature when I entered Moeller. I thought smart people got good grades, and bad people were the ones in jail. I thought that is how the world worked when I entered high school.

As I proceeded through my education at Moeller, I maintained decent grades, but learned more important lessons in the process. I learned that everyone is so different, and no one can be generalized. I learned that when I treat others how I want to be treated, it might work or not, but I did my part. Those who responded positively I began to pursue relationships with, and those who responded negatively, I did not. I knew they wanted to be nice, but there was something about them I probably didn't understand. I also realized that people are not always the person I see every day, but may be hiding behind something. I've struggled to realize if that is my job, to try and help those people, or simply let them figure it out like I did. I began to develop pretty close friends that I had not known three years earlier. I was amazed at the concept of a new friendship. It had been so long for me to remember what a NEW friendship was like. I started to see the majority of the class as individuals instead of the people I didn't go to grade school with. I really started to enjoy my participation at Moeller. The epitome of when I felt the most unified in my class at Moeller was the state basketball game in Columbus versus Shaker Heights, a team heavily favored to win. The emotions, the unity, the excitement of winning our first state basketball title made me feel like I was almost the one who received the alley-oop pass to slam the game-clincher home. I felt I was out there along with the entire student body. I will never forget that.

Looking back, I will always remember that I am not always right and I should listen to everyone's opinion in search for the best result. Maturity is the acceptance of your faults, I believe, and then dealing with these faults. I will always remember how it feels to be made fun of, excluded, so that I may be able to help those who feel excluded. I have used those instances only to make me stronger. I know that not necessarily all over-achievers have it together, and have problems just like under-achievers. I like that the main thing I have learned about life while at Moeller can be summed up in three sentences: All people are unique and have distinct personalities, but all deserving of equal respect. Do not judge other lest you be judged. Treat your neighbor as yourself. I never thought Bible quotes would ever be applicable to my own life, but I realize that I was being close-minded to familiarity again. It's funny, most people want to be known or popular, but I wanted to be common. I eventually broke out of that ideal and became a pretty well-known figure on campus. I will take all that I have learned at Moeller and use it to help me succeed, and the hallowed hallways of Moeller have produced another man, John Medl.

2 ENTRY 2

THIS IS A LETTER I WROTE TO THE CINCINNATI-BASED NON-PROFIT organization, 1N5.org. Their mission is to stop the stigma surrounding mental illness through advocacy. They have fundraisers and share stories of people who are fighting the battle of mental illness. They have a website and can also be found all across social media.

To Whom It May Concern,

I hope that sharing my story helps others within your organization. I was first diagnosed with bipolar disorder with psychotic features in 2006. Since then, I have been diagnosed with panic disorder/generalized anxiety disorder, post traumatic stress disorder, obsessive-compulsive disorder, agoraphobia, and claustrophobia. I have dedicated my life to helping others, spreading awareness, and ending stigma. I have a social media page, for which I am the administrator named "Mental Health Awareness and Online Support". I am also a published poet at maverickmagazine.com. Both are free resources for anyone interested. I have written 3 books, with my newest book just published titled, "The Last Day of July: 13 Years of Madness". All 3 books are available on online. Thanks for your time in reading my story.

Sincerely,
John E. Medl

3 ENTRY 3

This next entry was when I was reflecting on my life on my 38th birthday in October 2019.

38 things I've learned in the last 38 years:

1. Love is the most powerful force on Earth
2. Most things we worry about don't matter
3. Kindness is never the wrong thing to do
4. You don't have to be rich to be charitable and generous
5. Broad social change starts with an individual. (Thanks, Prof. Connelly)
6. Every day has the potential to be a good day
7. A loving family and good friends are priceless
8. The world is full of good people. If you can't find one, be one.
9. People who put you down don't like something about themselves

10. The world is changed by your example, not your opinion
11. Apologize whenever necessary
12. Everyone runs this race we call life at all different paces
13. Money can be a great thing, but don't let it run your life
14. Being positive and having a grateful heart really helps in tough situations
15. The world is full of suffering, but it is also full of people overcoming it
16. Recovery from tragedy is not linear
17. Perfection is not an option
18. There are many varieties of intelligence
19. If you tell the truth, you don't have to remember anything
20. Even the smartest person on the planet only knows a small amount of all there is to know
21. Dream big
22. Don't let mistakes define you
23. You don't get an award for being right. Sometimes, it's worth it to walk away from arguments.
24. Forgiveness is an attribute of the strong.
25. Sometimes a kick in the teeth is what you need at the time
26. Never give up; there is dignity in fighting
27. Integrity is doing the right thing even when no one is looking
28. Fix the cause. Not just the symptoms.
29. Practice your craft. You will statistically get better.

30. A career is a job. A vocation is a calling.
31. The thing people will remember most about you is how you treated them.
32. It is not any of our jobs to judge others
33. Everyone you meet is fighting a battle you know nothing about
34. You meet everyone for a reason
35. Not everyone you lose is a loss
36. Eat, drink, and be merry
37. Prayer never hurts
38. You only get so many birthdays

4 ENTRY 4

This next entry is a letter I wrote to home bound senior citizens for Christmas.

Hello, I hope this card brightens your day and your holidays! My name is John, and I attended St. Saviour school for all 8 years, and then Moeller High School and The University of Dayton. I wanted to send you a Christmas card to let you know that there are so many people that care about you and are praying for you this Christmas season. I'm hoping for a white Christmas, but I don't have to travel. I hope you have plenty of loved ones to share the season with, and if you don't, this card is a reminder that people care about you, even people you have never met before. MERRY CHRISTMAS!

5 ENTRY 5

I WAS GIVEN A SIGNED BASEBALL BY THE COMMISSIONER OF MAJOR League Baseball after I wrote him this letter.

Dear Commissioner Manfred,

I would like to request an autographed baseball from you. I'm not exactly sure if that is how it works. It seems very generous of you. I collect Cincinnati sports memorabilia, so that's why I am interested in an autographed baseball. I will include my address at the end of this letter. If you can't oblige, that's okay. I will just tell you a few of my thoughts about baseball. I was lucky to play on a little league team for ten years when I was a child. I am thirty-three years old now. Those were the best times of my life. My dad and I watch every Cincinnati Reds game that is available on TV/Cable. It's one of the only things we have always had in common.

I really like what you have done for the speed of the game. The games go much quicker, but not too fast. I know people get touchy when you start talking about changing in general, but the rules of baseball more so. I think you are doing a fantastic job with suspensions and penalties as well. Criminals, PEDs, and any form of cheating belittles the integrity of the game and should not be tolerated.

I would not be a good Reds fan (for my whole life) unless I give a mention to Pete Rose being allowed to be on the ballot for the Hall of Fame. I know you know that many players, former and current, have done much worse. I think the man has done his time for his crimes against baseball. Regardless, he is the greatest hitter of all time. No one can take that away from him. It would be nice if he took his rightful spot in the Hall with all the other greats.

There is a topic that is near and dear to my heart that I need to mention too. That's mental illness. I was diagnosed with bipolar disorder in 2006, and since then, Obsessive Compulsive Disorder, Panic Disorder, Generalized Anxiety Disorder, and agoraphobia have been added to my complete diagnosis. I have not seen a night in baseball in any stadium devoted to mental illness, and to the people who are suffering and the ones we have lost to suicide. I know it is not a happy topic, but it would be great if MLB could do something for one night in every stadium. A lime green ribbon is our symbol. The statistics are staggering for how common mental illness is. I believe that as many as one in three people have some type of mental illness. I volunteer my time every day to a social media page that I created for mental illness awareness. I am also a published author of my life story titled, "Millions Like Me: My Struggle with Mental Illness". I am a published poet at maverickmagazine.com as well. Thank you so much for your time and devotion to the betterment of the game.

Sincerely,
John E. Medl

6 ENTRY 6

MANY YEARS AGO, I HIT A PARKED CAR GOING ABOUT 10MPH. Nothing bad happened, but they took me by ambulance to the hospital to get checked out. I had about two beers and I took a hit or two off a joint. They did a blood test to check for drugs, and nothing significant showed up.

I was sitting there with two African-American police officers, and I kinda had the munchies, and I said, "Do you have anything to eat around here?"

One of the cops said, "We might have some juice or crackers".

So I said, "What did you call me?"

We all had a good laugh.

7 ENTRY 7

I HAVE TO SEE THE DOCTOR TODAY, WHICH IS USUALLY unpleasant, but I feel pretty good today. I've been upset about this appointment for weeks. Luckily, I was able to still enjoy the holidays the best I could, although I'm not much of a festive person. I'm lucky that I have a doctor I like, and we are on a first name basis. He reminds me of a "bro"....maybe someone I would be friends with outside of the clinical setting. He is very proud of me, and he's very easygoing and easy to talk to. I have some good news to tell him today, but I also have a lot of questions about my progress. I am getting to the point where my anxiety when leaving the house is too much to bear, and I have extreme irritability on a fairly regular basis. I don't know how much I can expect from my brain and body, which really is the whole mystery about mental illness. It's a lot of trial and error, whether it be medication or cognitive therapy. There's no road map, and there's no magic pill. Some of the work has to be done by the patient (me). Right now, I have high anxiety when leaving the house and low energy, almost always. I want to see if that can be improved, either with a medicine change or other cognitive therapy. One thing is for sure: I have fought the whole time. It's one of my redeeming qualities. I hope when my life is over that being a fighter is one of the main things people remember about me, followed by how much I loved and gave to others.

8 ENTRY 8

I HAVEN'T DONE MUCH JOURNALING SINCE I FINISHED MY LAST book in July 2019, which has been a nice break, but I wanted to share a few things today about my progress and mental illness in general. I have to see my doctor today, who simply wants me to call him Ben. Really awesome, younger guy. Very smart, kind, and approachable. I really like him as my doctor. It's going to be a great feeling when I hand him a copy of my new book. He was very impressed that I had written so much last time I saw him. It seemed like he was just generally impressed by the work I do, and my insight into my illness.

I'm glad the day of my appointment is finally here, so I know that it will all be over by this afternoon. I'm in better shape, anxiety-wise than usual, and overall, it is getting easier to see the doctor now that I am on a 3 month schedule rather than every month. Within the last few years, I used to have major anxiety and panic attacks at the doctor. My chest hurt and my head felt foggy every time I saw the doctor. I used to have to steady myself against the wall sometimes just to keep my balance.

One thing I want to say about mental illness is that there's no real clear cut objectives. No finish line or deadlines for improvement. Yes, things like taking a shower, driving, and socializing have gotten easier for me, and I guess that's because I kept trying. When I drove myself downtown the other day, that was a major accomplishment, but there's no guarantee that I can do it today or tomorrow. It's all so subjective and case-by-case. I know people with bipolar disorder that have full-time careers. That is not possible for me right now. If I was in proper shape, mentally and physically, I would try to apply for a career other than writing. It's just frustrating that there's no end game. Am I a success now? I would say yes. Is it possible that I could return to work eventually? Probably, but again, there's no guarantees. Just wanted to share my thoughts for a minute.

9 ENTRY 9

When I saw the doctor yesterday, I was totally ready to change my medications, as scary as that idea sounded. I talked to my doctor, and he was actually happy with my progress. He told me he took the time to read through my medical records (over 13 years' worth) and my books, and I really have come a long way. Like almost miraculous. I feel pretty good most of the time. It's at least tolerable. I don't expect to feel perfect all the time. I told him a lot of feelings and thoughts I have, and he basically pointed out that I overthink a lot of things, which I kinda already knew. He told me I have to find ways to turn my brain off, per se. Music, crossword puzzles, whatever works. Writing about all of this really helps me, and I know it helps others as well. Another part of shutting down my brain is taking time for myself to recharge my batteries before I do too much advocating. Everything I do doesn't have to be for a cause or to help others. The doctor was more concerned with my mood being stable and that I was getting enough sleep. He wasn't even concerned that I gained 12 pounds, but I am. I have to work on that. I'm still down 38 pounds overall, however, so I'm not starting from scratch. My BP was 138/88, which I have no idea what that means, but I know it's always high at the doctor's office. My pulse is always elevated, too. I had a brief panic attack when I got in my mom's van to go to the appointment, but I got out, and took some deep breaths, and I was able to keep the appointment. I'm really glad it's over until almost April. I found that riding in the back seat helps, for whatever reason. Maybe because I'm not right up on the dash or something. He recommended therapy (CBT) for my cognition, but I'm still thinking if I want to make that commitment. It was nice to be reminded that I have made so much progress, but I'm also looking forward to the challenge of improving little things in my life that might make a big difference.

10 ENTRY 10

THIS IS A LETTER I WROTE TO ELLEN DEGENERES, AND I INCLUDED a copy of my first book. I think this was sometime around 2014.

Hi Ellen! (Ms. DeGeneres is probably more appropriate, but it doesn't feel right. I think of you as such a kind, humble person)

Here is a copy of my book. It's my life story, detailing my struggle with mental illness. I have been diagnosed with bipolar disorder with psychotic features, generalized anxiety disorder/panic disorder, post traumatic stress disorder, claustrophobia, and agoraphobia. I would be honored if you just gave it a read. I remember watching your sitcom as a younger adult, and it was hilarious. As I started watching your talk show, I saw again how funny you are, but I also saw such a humble, happy, and kind soul. Thanks for any time you give me.

Love and Best Wishes,
John Edward Medl
johnmedl7@gmail.com

11 ENTRY 11

I HOPE YOU FIND THIS AS FUNNY AS I DO.... THE DYNAMIC OF MY household goes like this—Mom pretty much controls the household and knows everything that's going on. My dad has veto power, but in a limited capacity. I am the low man on the totem pole, and I try to just mind my own business and keep to myself whenever possible. All of us get along fairly well, all things considered, UNTIL the balance of power is messed with. All of this leads me to the day when my dad said something so funny to my mom. My mom was trying to tell my dad what clothes to wear or that he needed a jacket or something, and my dad was just like, "I think I can do what I want". Wrong thing to say to Queen Bee! LOL

12 ENTRY 12

I HAVE BEEN TO MANY HOOKAHVILLES, STARTING AROUND 1998. Hookahville is a weekend-long music festival where the band Ekoostik Hookah is the main act. My last Hookahville was Spring 2006, or whichever one that was when Blues Traveler was there. I used to go to all kinds of concerts, but I was diagnosed with bipolar disorder and anxiety, so I don't leave my house much, and large crowds intimidate me. Well, I decided to step outside my comfort zone and go see my friends' band, The Summit, (with Ekoostik Hookah) around November of last year. My buddy, Mike Hennel, (drummer for The Summit), introduced me to Eric, the drummer for Hookah. I told Eric a little about my story and he asked if I had any requests. I honestly couldn't believe Eric was even asking me. When I was growing up, Hookah were some of my heroes. You never really think of ever meeting them or connecting with them on a personal level. The only songs I could think of were Ohio Grown and Loner. Sure enough, right as I was about to leave (early) for the night, Hookah played Loner! I like to believe it was for me :) Much love to you all! (Hookah later confirmed that the song Loner was, in fact, for me). What a great night.

13 ENTRY 13

Sometimes, it's our own bullshit that is holding us back. No one tries to trigger me or upset me. It just happens. It's hard to know how much I can actually control how I react. I have to train my mind to not worry and overthink so much, which is quite a battle. I have to work at it. The worst panic attack I've had in the last couple months was in the beginning of November 2019, and I was tempting the Fates. I drank coffee and didn't allow my medicine to work properly before getting in the car. I knew better. I don't know why I thought I could sneak something like that past my illness that day. Being successful takes extreme care, caution, maintenance, and constant attempts to improve.

14 ENTRY 14

I'VE BEEN FOOLISH LATELY, OR PERHAPS JUST HUMAN. I HAVE BEEN getting caught up in the struggle and stress of daily life, and I have been forgetting how blessed I am. I can't believe my life has turned out the way it has. Thank you all to everyone who has supported me in any way. I don't really know anyone with a mental illness who has as much support as I do, not that it's a competition, obviously. I have everything and everyone that I need, but the more good people the merrier.

15 ENTRY 15

Fear is a part of anxiety, but I wouldn't say I'm always scared when I have anxiety. I bring this up because I need to drive and run some errands today. Not an emergency or anything. My mom will run them for me if I can't do it. I'm lucky in that regard. But driving is so difficult for me because there is definitely a fear present, but I also have physical symptoms like numbness in my arms, dizziness, and chest pains. It's really hard for me to understand because I used to drive for a living. I guess I'm scared to drive because I don't want to cause an accident. I don't know if that's a reasonable concern or if I'm just guilty of over-thinking again. For me to successfully run errands, I have to shut down my mind enough to drive without a ton of worry, and I have to make sure my body is ready for the trip so that I don't get symptomatic while I'm driving. It would be easy if I could predict when all this is going to happen. It's just kind of a confident feeling and I guess a leap of faith that my medicine will work enough to drive. When I get excited about driving somewhere successfully, it really is an accomplishment for me. Sometimes, I just don't think people understand how bad it can be, and also I don't want others to feel ashamed if they struggle with driving too.

16 ENTRY 16

I LEFT MY LAST DOCTOR'S APPOINTMENT A FEW WEEKS AGO WITH A lot of things to work on and think about. My two main challenges right now are driving/leaving the house and overthinking. I've started to put together a Lego set, filling in crosswords, and trying to read, both for pleasure and education of my illnesses. I'm trying to improve my mood and patience with others. I always wonder how much I can actually control my reaction to things. I have an open relationship with my parents where I can say things like, "Give me a minute. It's time for my medication." and things of that nature. My weight has been a battle my whole life, so I'm always trying to improve my physical health, mainly through weight loss. I am doing a better job of that since the holidays have passed. I only weigh myself a few times a year, but I can tell by how my clothes fit. I would like to start walking in my neighborhood. Hopefully, I can get up the energy and motivation when it's warmer outside, but if it's cold and if it's time, I will walk in the cold. I am even smoking less and drinking less coffee. I have extreme OCD when it comes to my medication times, and I still refuse to take my medicine early, but I have relaxed and allowed to take them later than scheduled. It's a trick of mine to have more energy, but I would never skip a dose entirely, on purpose anyway. Journaling like this has always helped me cope, and I probably have enough material for another book, but I'm not planning on doing that. I might look for a writing job somewhere. "The medicine works" my doctor tells me, so I tell myself that when I don't feel great. It really is amazing how far I've come. I have a lot to work on, but I'm in a great position to do whatever I want to do with my life from here on out. I'm grateful and blessed in many ways.

17 ENTRY 17

I GOT A SMALL SHIPMENT OF MY OLDER TWO BOOKS TODAY. I WILL be getting another shipment of my newest book on February 4, 2020. I always enjoy autographing them all. It's a personal touch, and I feel like a part of me goes with every copy. My super secret wish is that my signature would be worth money some day, and my friends could sell my books for a lot of money. I used to practice my signature in grade school because I dreamed of being a professional baseball player. I dreamed of signing baseballs and roaring fans in a packed stadium. I guess a writer is close enough haha. I just don't think I was meant to be rich because I don't love money enough. When I have money, the greatest joy I get is to share it. It's part of my desire to help others and make other people happy. There are downsides to having that kind of personality, but overall, it has worked out for me. I was able to drive my car again to give it some work with no real issues, and I had a nice dinner with my parents. I finished my Lego set I was working on, and I'm almost finished with my article for The Antioch Review that's due at the end of February. Just writing about some pleasant thoughts that I had this evening.

18 ENTRY 18

I BELIEVE THAT MENTAL ILLNESS IS MOSTLY A GENETIC predisposition that comes to the surface after a variety of environmental factors take place. It would be hard to pinpoint exactly what led to my diagnosis(es), but most of it had nothing to do with anything I did wrong morally or otherwise. I guess what I am getting at is that it doesn't help myself or anyone else to beat myself up for past behavior or feel sorry for myself. I try not to fall into that trap. I have work to do, and I can't accomplish treatment goals or help others if I am constantly looking back and wondering what I could have done differently. The past is over. There's very literally nothing I can do about it now, so I have to ask myself 'Now what?'. My medication helps calm my symptoms, but I have to do a lot of the work myself to gain progress. I am testing my anxiety every day, more and more, and I have had some great results. What did I have to lose? A panic attack? I've survived hundreds of those. Whenever I try to leave the house, most of the time every signal in my body is telling me "No, you can't do that". My brain is sending fear signals. I guess at some point I made a leap of faith that my medication will work and the fear would go away. If you are stuck in your progress, ask yourself what you have to lose. My memory isn't very good, but in the past year, I have made a lot of progress, and I have gained so much. If you have severe anxiety or other mental illness, please keep trying. It can get better. I can't promise you anything, but it has gotten better for me. I don't know how to give away that resiliency that comes with not giving up. All I can do is try to be a good example and tell you what has worked for me and that my life has gotten better. I never quit on anyone.

19 ENTRY 19

Only a few people in my circle on social media talk about mental illness, and I only know them in a professional capacity. It helps me to talk about my illness because it helps others, which in turn, helps me. It makes me feel like my struggles are all worth it. So, I just want to mention that people "let themselves go" for a variety of reasons, but it tends to happen a lot with people with mental illness. Hygiene can be a big challenge, which includes things like taking a shower, weight control, and other personal cleanliness. I have lost over 50 pounds now, and of course I'm proud of myself, but I have a long ways to go before I really feel like I'm at a healthy weight. I think it's important to celebrate small successes along the way, but I try not to get too comfortable. I'm not really ready to declare victory over my illness, and I probably never will. I am always on high alert for triggers and red flags, which may sidetrack my progress. I fail sometimes, but I always try to put forth the best effort I can. I took a shower this morning and did some personal grooming. I also went out to lunch with my mom. All of these things are victories over my illness in that I both couldn't do them before, and that these tasks are still hard for me. I guess what I am getting at is that I'm starting to feel better mentally/psychologically, so I hope it will be easier for me to lose weight and take better care of myself physically. Just trying to hang tough, live right, and do the right thing.

20 ENTRY 20

I drove myself downtown again. I'm so proud of myself and just so grateful and happy (not always). If some of you knew what I have bounced back from, you would be amazed. My recovery and recent success is really something special. The best gift that mental illness gave me was appreciating every little success along the way. This is a lifelong illness. There is no cure. I am going to have to manage it the rest of my life, but when I can enjoy life at the same time, the struggles don't seem so bad. I have made so much progress!

21 ENTRY 21

When I think of authors, I think about people like Stephen King and James Patterson, but not myself, for some reason. When I was a kid, authors of books that I read were just otherworldly or something. I never thought I would become one, especially three times over. I am lucky to know some amazing authors and writers, and they have taught me a lot. I always think that I couldn't be a writer for a living, but here I am, writing again. I've thought about getting my MA in Counseling or doing some public speaking too. This whole journey has been very surreal in a lot of ways.

When strangers meet me, a lot of the time, they say it seems like they have known me for years. I think I'm pretty transparent. What you see is what you get. Maybe it's good vibes or something. A lot of people confide in me, which is a compliment that people trust me so much with their life stories. I very rarely get overwhelmed with all of it. I just feel like this is what I am supposed to be doing right now. I haven't changed too much, and if I have, I would like to think I'm just a better version of my old self. I'm always trying to improve myself, and every day, I am getting better at coping with mental illness. I am surrounded by so many people that love me. It really helps me deal with life. It's also a pretty amazing feeling to think that I am helping others by simply telling my story, perhaps even saving lives. I've come so far.

22 ENTRY 22

I HOPE I HAVE MADE A POSITIVE IMPACT ON YOUR LIFE IN SOME capacity. You probably don't have to read my books to know a lot about my story. If you aren't feeling well mentally, please reach out. There's the crisis line, or even calling the police or an ambulance. You can reach out to me, but I can only help so much if you need medical attention. I've lost a few friends to suicide and drug overdoses, and I want it to stop. 10-20% of bipolar sufferers die by suicide, and 50% have attempted suicide. One in five people have a mental illness. These are staggering numbers when considered to scale of the general population. I know I can't save everyone, but no one is going to stop me from trying. I guess I am a little greedy in that I want to have an impact on more than one person because a lot of people say, "If I could just help one person..." I want to help a lot of people, and I hope my story is read and told for many years after I expire.

23 ENTRY 23

I WILL HAVE 7 MORE COPIES OF MY NEWEST BOOK AROUND September 24, 2019. Around that time, I will be shipping a variety of my books to NAMI (National Alliance for Mental Illness) in New Mexico, totaling around 10 copies. Thanks to my readers, friends, family, and even strangers who love and support me. It truly makes a difference. If I hear that I'm doing the right thing from others, it seems like life has been treating me well, which I take as a sign from the universe that I am doing the right thing. I am wise and humble enough to not declare victory just yet over my illness. It's going to be a life-long battle. I hope I am up to the challenge. So far, so good I guess. Whatever mental illness has taken from me, I have gotten back exponentially, and I am grateful and blessed.

24 ENTRY 24

I'VE HAD 2 PANIC ATTACKS IN THE LAST TWO DAYS, AND SOME general anxiety. The panic attacks are less than a minute usually, but I was hyperventilating, which I haven't experienced in some time. General anxiety can last much longer. For me, it lasts until I eat a meal and take a nap. Mental illness is not fair, nor is life. I miss out on a lot of things to remain stable. If you think mental illness is "all in our heads", you are simply wrong and don't understand mental illness. I hope you never have to understand. It's physical, emotional, and psychological. It's a daily struggle to remain stable. I am physically sore and exhausted from the panic and anxiety. I had planned to go see my friends' band play today, but I simply don't feel up to it. I had been planning on it for months.

A panic attack that lasts a minute can bruise my ego and confidence. One minute is all it takes for me to be less confident about my progress. I am kind of a veteran of panic and anxiety, so I know I just have to build my confidence up again. I also know that a meal and a nap will take care of the problem. Just a little disappointed today, but I'm sure it will be better after I rest.

25 ENTRY 25

I don't know if this is a surprise to anyone, but I'm not that confident of a writer. Sometimes I think people are just being nice when they buy my books. Maybe they believe in supporting local artists. All of that is great, and I appreciate the support, but when you delve into my books, you will find more than a little valuable information about mental illness. My second book was a poetry book, which was more my creative side, but my first book is very clinical, and my third book is journal style, detailing life with mental illness. I say that my books have value because it's just an amazing story. Not a lot of people talk about mental illness, and a lot don't even survive for a variety of reasons. Then, for someone like me to have a clear enough mind to write about all of it. It's just a rare thing.

26 ENTRY 26

I FEEL RAGE SOMETIMES. IT'S NOT RATIONAL ANGER. IT'S NOT ME, but I can get fixated on something I don't like about life, or I can feel rage for seemingly no reason at all. Usually, it is when my medicine hasn't started working yet. I feel awful when I am mean to my parents, but they know it's not me acting out. They know it's not in my character. I always apologize if I think I was being irrational too. I have some things in place that I do that help ease my anger/rage until it passes. I want to share because maybe these techniques will help you:

I go into a quiet room. If I feel like listening to music, I put on relaxing music, emphasis on relaxing. Sometimes, I close my eyes and just breathe in and out in silence. I roll my own cigarettes, so that monotonous action helps calm me and helps spend unnecessary anger energy. I sit on my porch and have a cigarette, and watch the traffic go by. I try to think of myself as separate from the race everyone is running. I might text a friend and ask that person how their day went. I might crack jokes on social media to help cheer me up. I might go out of my way to be kind to someone else.

I am basically trying to distract myself and my rage long enough for the medicine to work. Rage is rare for me, but it's a strong emotion that I have. I absolutely hate it because it's not in my character or personality. I have a hard time being mean to people that deserve it, much less for no reason. Also, journaling like this helps too.

27 ENTRY 27

For the longest time, I thought I was jealous of people who can drink alcohol all the time, have a good time, and still function. That's not it. Alcohol and drugs have and always will be there for me if I choose. Stability, productivity, sanity, and peace of mind were gone from my life for a long time, and I have been fighting very hard to get it all back. These are the qualities that I lost and that I value so much. I don't value being fucked up anymore. I don't need to self-medicate because my medicine works most of the time. I have slip ups. I had 5 beers about a week ago, and I had a good time actually, but I'm playing with fire. Shit man, I'm playing with fire when I have something as harmless as coffee. Maybe I have more to lose now than I did before, because stability, sanity, and all those great qualities are priceless to me. I'm not willing to risk a night of drunkenness for everything I have fought for. Overall, I'm doing a pretty good job, all things considered.

28 ENTRY 28

Every so often, I like to thank my whole support team, which includes my readers, family, and friends. It makes a world of difference in my fight to stay positive and stable with my illness. Kindness matters. A few months ago, a woman at the grocery deli called me fat to someone she was talking to on her phone. I still think about it. It hurt a little bit emotionally, but I know I am doing the best I can to control my weight, and I also know I have been big my whole life. My point is that this woman probably had no idea the physical, emotional, and mental strength it took me to drive myself to the grocery. This was a time when driving for me was near impossible, and social interactions made me extremely anxious. She also didn't know that I had $5 to my name, and all I wanted was my favorite pasta salad to treat myself. Would she have cared had she known all of that? Maybe, but probably not. The world has gotten more unkind over the years, in my opinion. A lot of people have a psychological need to put others down to make themselves feel better about their own lives, which they are probably unsatisfied with, hence this psychological need to put others down. "In a world where you can be anything, be kind". Simple words from Dr. Seuss, but it can make a huge difference. I am lucky and blessed to have so many who support me and my writing. I care more about others being comforted by my story than any amount of money I make off my books. I donate them whenever I can. If you think my story is disturbing or outstanding or tragic or whatever, you should see some of the cases of people who have no support. So, a simple thank you to all of you. I would like to take credit individually for my successes, but I am not much of a success without all of your support. I think of myself as a humble servant or vessel just carrying out a mission.

29 ENTRY 29

My attitude has been pretty shitty off and on lately, and that's on me. It's a little more challenging to control my emotional reaction to things because of my illness, but I'm not the guy who likes excuses. I drove to the tobacco store today, which is only a few miles away, but I didn't have much anxiety. I was worried that I was relapsing or something, which would have been devastating to my confidence. I can't tell you how annoying it is for me to have to wait almost an hour to be calm enough to drive, BUT I'm thankful I have a car and that I can drive at all because I used to pretty much be confined to the house. With me, it's all about perspective and gratitude, and I lose sight of everything I'm blessed with sometimes. I'm a good person, and I know it, but I'm not perfect, and I know that too. No one is.

30 ENTRY 30

My illness has changed me in many ways, some for the better, and some for the worse. I would like to think more for the better. I have trouble relating to a lot of people because they just don't have an illness to contend with on a daily basis, so their priorities and outlook are different from mine. I really just want to make a difference through my books and otherwise, and be happy most of the time. Anything above that is great too. I've had more money than I could spend, and I was definitely happy. I bought a bunch of stuff I didn't need and went to bars and bought everyone drinks. I had a great time, but I didn't save a dime. I learned my lesson, I guess. I still have trouble budgeting money, but it's not like I have some kind of million dollar trust fund to work with. I know that the white picket fence idea is not for me, at least not for the time being. I guess I understand the draw to that kind of life, but I'm selfish with my time and energy, and I'm not willing to share it with anyone right now in a relationship kind of way. I have plenty of people who love me in a familial and friendly way to keep me busy with my love. I guess it's hard to explain, and I certainly don't owe anyone an explanation, but everything changed when I got sick.

31 ENTRY 31

My really good buddy called me out of the blue around midnight a few nights ago. He just felt the urge to give me a pep talk of sorts, which I didn't think I needed at the time, but I did. He told me that I have to let the things go that I've done that I'm not exactly proud of. He's right. I think my biggest regret is not what I've done or not done, it's how much energy and guilt I gave to my regrets, and how much I cared about what other people thought of me. All that really matters is who I am today, and I'm proud of that person. There's no need to beat myself for things that happened a long time ago. It's not fair to myself, and it's not productive if I want to help and love others. I think when we are young; we are taught to feel guilt and remorse for things we've done wrong, which is a good way to learn right from wrong, but at some point in our adult lives, we have to let it all go. I'm the only person I'm going to have to live with my whole life. I have to love and forgive myself, and I'm still learning.

32 ENTRY 32

My books and my writings about mental illness will never be popular or well circulated. There are many reasons for that. Most people simply don't care about mental illness at all. The ones who do care either have an illness or someone close to them has it. Even some people with loved ones who have mental illness don't care. Some people don't even believe in modern medicine to treat mental illness. But, oh don't people love to blame mental illness, especially mass shootings, since they somehow have become trendy and popular. Everyone is in denial that the US has a gun problem. People actually think that people like me want to take their guns. Most people, even in their right mind, aren't responsible enough to own guns. They are dangerous killing weapons. Some guns' sole purpose is to kill as many people in as short a time as possible. Oh, but it's the mentally ill that's the problem. It couldn't be the access to guns. Then you have people who suffer from mental illness who are ashamed to even talk about it. Gee, I wonder why. The mentally ill are demonized by most of society and pill shamed if they need to take medicine.

33 ENTRY 33

I TELL PEOPLE ALL THE TIME THAT THE BEST GIFT MENTAL ILLNESS has given to me is an appreciation for the little things (which maybe are big things) and a general sense of gratitude. I was never a bad person. I just didn't fully appreciate how blessed I was, and I took life for granted. I use the word blessed instead of lucky or fortunate because I feel like blessed is a superlative word, and that's the degree to which I feel the gratitude, if that makes sense. When I use the word blessed, I am basically just describing the overwhelming sense of gratitude that I feel quite often now.

34 ENTRY 34

My good buddy told me at my birthday party, "Just be you". Such a simple statement. This good friend thought that me being myself was good enough for him. I think we complicate things sometimes by always striving to be better and obtain more "stuff". There's nothing wrong with trying to better yourself and move up the money ladder, of course, but sometimes we define ourselves by status symbols and whatever else society says makes us good enough. Being myself is good enough for my friends, and that's actually an amazing thing, and takes a lot of pressure off me. I know how to be me. I can do that. I just want my friends to be themselves too. I wouldn't keep them around if I didn't think they were good, solid people. If you are a good person with good intentions, just be you. The world doesn't need more successful people (again, nothing is wrong with that). The world needs more good, kind, and loving people.

35 ENTRY 35

I'M REALLY PROUD OF MYSELF. I FOUGHT HARD TODAY. TODAY wasn't terrible, but it certainly wasn't easy. I had some anxiety and racing thoughts throughout the day, but I managed to do some housework, which helps calm me and also helps my mom. I shaved my face, which may seem very minor to most, but when I was first hospitalized in 2006, I had to earn the trust of the nurses to use a razor. Razors and sharp objects were only allowed by patients at the nurses' discretion for (hopefully) obvious reasons. I always think about the tiny drab community bathrooms and showers when I shave my face. Shaving my face is a reminder of the freedom I have earned in recovery, and it gives me a sense of pride every time I shave. I have traumatic memories from the hospital too, but shaving my face elicits mostly good feelings. I don't even take shaving my face for granted anymore. I am also budgeting money better this month and improving my general mood.

36 ENTRY 36

I USE SOCIAL MEDIA FOR A LOT OF THE SAME REASONS EVERYONE else does—sharing memes and photos, random status updates, etc. I definitely like to make people laugh, but I also like to use social media for a purpose. I run my own page devoted to mental health awareness, and it's a great tool for a small time author like me to promote my books. Social media has also allowed me to stay in contact with so many people when I was super sick. I also like all the live music venue feeds because I can't always be there in person.

37 ENTRY 37

I'M SITTING HERE LOOKING AT A PILE OF MY BOOKS THAT I ordered, and it's just such a wild feeling that I turned out to be an author/writer. When I got a degree in psychology, I thought I was going to be a psychologist. Being a writer was something so far from my plans. You may as well told me I was going to be an astronaut. Weird how stuff works out sometimes when you think it isn't. I'm helping at least as many people as I would have had I become a psychologist. It's just such a weird feeling to look at a book and know that I wrote it. I'm not trying to toot my own horn or anything. Just being honest.

38 ENTRY 38

My anxiety got the best of me just now. I tried 3 times to get into my mom's car to go get my truck from having repairs, and I couldn't sit still, and I had chest pains from anxiety. The reason I had an anxiety attack or whatever it was, was because I had just taken my medicine and it hadn't kicked in yet (usually takes about an hour or so). Luckily, my awesome parents picked up my car for me, so now I don't have to worry about it. I can't stress enough how important it is to have support with mental illness. I am truly blessed with great friends and family who I know are always going to be there for me. Others are not as fortunate, which is one of the big reasons I try to be a good example by fighting this illness and trying to be there for others. Usually, the best cure for a panic attack like that is a good meal and a nap, so that's what I'm going to do.

39 ENTRY 39

It really freaked me out when I couldn't sit still from panic and ride in my mom's car yesterday. I had a doctor's appointment scheduled for tomorrow, and I had to reschedule. I contacted my case manager, and I told him I wasn't feeling well or confident enough to endure a doctor's appointment tomorrow. Props to my case manager for responding to my texts when he was out of the office. I told my parents I wasn't feeling well too. That's all I can do I think. I'm a little upset because I feel like some of my progress was taken away, but hopefully, I will be okay shortly. It's been a lot worse before.

40 ENTRY 40

THE REASON I WRITE ABOUT MY STRUGGLES AND TRIUMPHS IS TO inspire others and make others feel like they are not alone. I'm not suffering. I struggle sometimes, and there's a big difference. I don't want anyone to feel sorry for me, but of course, I appreciate the support and prayers. I would rather you pray for people who are really suffering, but I guess there's enough to go around.

41 ENTRY 41

I'M NOT A BIG FAN OF DR. PHIL, BUT SOMETIMES MY DAD WATCHES his show because it's on TV right before the local news. He was talking to a 28-year-old female drug addict today, and he said something very powerful. He said, "You are 28 years old. You might have another 60 years on this planet. If you get help now, this could all just be a bad memory." What a wonderful thought for anyone who wants to change or put their past behind them. Maybe parts of my life can just be bad memories too, and I can move on (if I haven't already).

42 ENTRY 42

I'M GOING TO SELL HOWEVER MANY BOOKS, BUT I REALLY JUST want people to be inspired by my story. Maybe I can open some eyes as to what it's like to live with mental illness and how severe it can be, and how it's such a wide spectrum. Bills are bills, and money is money, but it doesn't matter to me if we have a chat about mental illness or you read about it in one of my books. It's just the same to me.

43 ENTRY 43

My driving anxiety has come back in the last week or so, but today, I drove to the library to submit my second book, "Poems from a Bipolar Mind" for their catalog. This book should be on the shelves in the next month or so. No anxiety issues at all, really. I was a little nervous when I left the house, but I'm really glad I was able to drive and get a little exercise. Anxiety and panic are only a little bit logical, so there's only so much that therapy can do. Usually, it's just a baby steps process to get back where I was, which I totally hate, but it is what it is. Just thankful I was able to overcome my fears today.

44 ENTRY 44

I JUST WENT TO WHITE CASTLE, AND THEY WERE SHORT 2 workers. They called off. Happens all the time in food service. Knowing this, instead of choosing to be angry and frustrated, I chose to just be happy that I was getting food that I was cheating on my diet. I was making conversation with other people in line and smiling. I also gave the cashier a $5 bill and thanked her for showing up. We make lots of choices every day. Choose to be the bigger person and the exception to the rule. Maybe on another day, I would have been upset. I don't know. I just think today was the day to show compassion and humility to these human beings who were serving me food.

45 ENTRY 45

I HAVE A MEETING WITH MY CASE MANAGER TODAY. HE HELPS ME a little bit with cognitive therapy, but mainly, he helps me fill out all the long, confusing paperwork associated with my illness. He was a Green Beret, which I think is cool, so I will have to wish him a belated Happy Veterans' Day. He was shot in the back in combat, and he's had back problems ever since. I think he fought around the time of the Vietnam War. I don't have to see the doctor until January 6th, so another "fun" thing I have to do is get my medication refills approved so that I have enough medication until I see the doctor.

You have no idea how many times I've wanted to say to my doctor, "Okay, I'm ready for the good shit" haha.

46 ENTRY 46

"THE ROBBED THAT SMILES STEALS SOMETHING FROM THE THIEF" IS a Shakespearean quote that I've always liked. I thought about going so far as to get it tattooed on me. I feel like when I have a positive attitude and sense of humor in the face of mental illness (The thief, if you will), I feel like I am getting something back that mental illness stole from me. Mental illness took everything I had at the time, and then it tried to take my life. I have survived over 13 years since those days many years ago. Looking back on my journey, a lot of people would call it a success story. I don't know about all that, but I'm definitely proud of how I have handled everything and how my life has turned out.

47 ENTRY 47

I'm always looking for natural ways to alleviate my bipolar and anxiety symptoms, and I read that singing out loud can help anxiety. This might explain why I don't have many problems singing karaoke, but why I still have problems driving to the bar to get there. Sometimes, I sing around the house without even thinking about it. Just a fun and weird thing about anxiety. I should say MY anxiety because what works for one person might not work for another. That's why mental illness is so hard to treat, whether with cognitive therapy and/or medication. Everyone experiences mental illness differently.

48 ENTRY 48

Sometimes, life can be overwhelming, and I let it get to me, and other times, I laugh at the magnitude of it all and my very small part in all of it. I laugh at all the dumb jokes I know or, ironically, the daily tasks when they seem never-ending. Of all the atoms that could have formed anything, a tiny fraction made me and you. Yes, I know the science. The fertilized egg, yada yada yada. But there still had to be a pretty incredible happening to form your being. Don't waste it. Have something to offer to others. As far as I know and believe, we only get one shot at this thing, so make it memorable. I always keep love and kindness in my heart, which I think helps me deal with a lot of things. Oh yeah, and as much comedy as I can fit into a day without annoying others.

49 ENTRY 49

I THINK BY THE TIME YOU GET TO BE MY AGE; YOU HAVE experienced some kind(s) of heartbreak and trauma that has left you a different person, if you are wise. I wish for myself that I have become a more grateful person, and a better all around person since I was first diagnosed. I lost everything—my house, my car, my mind, my reputation—literally everything. I have spent so much time trying to get my life back on track, with a lot of success. I never thought I would be an author and writer. I have touched many lives and helped many people, and that makes me happy and gives me purpose and the will to continue the journey. My mission in life has almost nothing to do with longevity, but rather making an impact. I'm not planning on going anywhere any time soon, but then again, no one really ever does. I want my life to be a celebration like the stupid birthday parties I have been throwing for about 10 years. I'm never going to be confident enough to say that I beat my illness, but it certainly didn't beat me.

50 ENTRY 50

My medicine is designed to keep my mood and behavior somewhere in the middle of the mood and behavioral spectrum, and it does for the most part, but it results in this murky indifference and numbness. If I ever feel emotions like sadness or happiness, they are usually to the extreme, and usually accompanied by anxiety. I absolutely hate being in a bad mood, and I try to do things that make me happy to get out of that mindset. I enjoy lots of things—reading, music, watching sports, talking with friends, acts of kindness, etc. etc. etc. Most of the time, these things help my bad mood, but I have a feeling I don't experience emotions like most people. There's no concrete way to know, but I know a lot of people, and they don't seem to have the same emotional spectrum as I do. Just something interesting I've observed about my illness.

51 ENTRY 51

I will see the doctor in a few weeks. I'm starting to think about what I want to talk to him about, and it's frustrating. I feel like I should want to do things, but I'm not interested in a lot of things. My energy level is low, and I'm sore from being overweight and inactive for a few months. It looks like depression symptoms, but I'm not really sad. I had enough energy to write my third book, but I don't think it would take this long to recover. For a few months, I was going out and driving and really enjoying myself. When the time and weather changed, and I had a massive panic attack. It was like the rug got pulled out from under me again. It's so frustrating. I finally have enough money to do things and maybe take a trip somewhere, but I can barely drive up the street. Bipolar disorder is episodic, which is a hope I am holding onto right now, and that this is just another phase. I'm very grateful that I got out and drove places when I could. I always try to seize those moments when I feel well because lately I haven't been able to do much.

52 ENTRY 52

Even the best of us get fed up—I'm sick of all the paperwork that goes along with being on government assistance. I'm sick of doctor's appointments and medications. I'm sick of being sober because I'm so worried about everyone else's health, and if something happened when I was drinking, I would feel completely awful. I would lose so much progress, but again, I'm worried about how my actions affect others. I think that a night out with my friends would solve these frustrations, or maybe even just a nice meal and nap, but don't think that I don't get upset and angry about all of this. I've been compliant ever since I entered treatment, but it's not my nature at all. I just hope I can settle down enough to continue to be on every else's time and schedules. I try my best to not complain and be a good boy and comply, but trust me, I want to break free of everything sometimes.

53 ENTRY 53

Many years ago, when I was in an emergency situation, my instincts and survival mode kicked in. And some sort of amazing pain tolerance that I have no idea where that came from. I don't really see surviving the emergencies I've had as courageous. What took courage was facing the aftermath each time, and dealing with mental illness day after day, week after week, year after year. I may have given up if I didn't have some solid support from family, friends, and readers of my books. I mention this because a few people have stopped by lately just to see me, and one of my friends brought me some homemade food. I just want people to know that kindness and support like this matter to people with mental illness, and I would think anyone, really. So many people don't have this kind of support, and that makes a negative difference, too. I don't really know what my point is here. I guess I just want to say that the support I have has helped me greatly, and if you are able, be that support for others. It matters.

54 ENTRY 54

Here's my funny story for the day to make you laugh. My mom will probably kill me, but oh well, I'll just unfriend her on social media again haha. So....I've only been to the strip club as a patron a few times. Not really my thing. But when I was working as a pizza delivery driver in Dayton, Ohio, we delivered to 3 strip clubs in our area. One night, I got such a delivery to a place called Pizazz (lol). Not classy at all. As soon as I walked through the door, I was in the middle of everything. I bring a pizza over to these 3 businessmen type people, and they tell me to sit down and have a drink with them. First of all, I wasn't old enough to drink, and secondly, I was driving all night. When I turned down the drinks, they gave me a $10 tip and told me to sit down and called over a stripper. They explained to me that I was going to get a lap dance too, whether I liked it or not. They didn't have to twist my arm or anything, but I felt so awkward because I'm pretty shy about this kind of thing. To make it even more awkward, when the stripper is doing her thing, she says, "MMM, you smell like pizza" WTF? I have no idea what I'm supposed to say. 'Oh yeah baby, it's a meat lovers'. I can get you pizza all night long. LOL. Anyway, hope that made you laugh. True story, of course.

55 ENTRY 55

THERE WAS A COURAGEOUS WOMAN FROM MY AREA WHO WAS diagnosed with a fatal brain injury. In her last days, all she wanted was letters of hope. Here is the letter I wrote to her. She played basketball for a college called Mount St. Joseph's, and scored a basket in one of her final days.

Dear Lauren,

There is so much I want to say to you. I wish I could just talk to you over coffee or something. I also hope you get this message. You are such a hero to so many people, including myself. I hope you realize how big of an impact your story has had on everyone, near and far. You have shown everyone how to face adversity with dignity and courage. You have turned a negative into a positive. Even that is such an understatement. Your story will be told for such a long time. That is something so special. Your impact is on the same level as famous authors, scientists, and dignitaries. My friends and family are praying for you, and we all wish you a Merry Christmas! Keep fighting!

Love,
John Edward Medl, Age 33 Cincinnati

56 ENTRY 56

WEIRD HAPPENINGS ON THE PORCH THIS MORNING... A MAN stopped his car in front of my house and started walking towards the porch. I thought it was my overdue package, but it was a guy my age who lived in the neighborhood. He said he drives by every day, and he saw me sleeping one day, and he wanted to make sure I was okay. He said it had been bothering him for a week because he didn't know if I was okay. I explained to him that I fall asleep sometimes on the porch because I'm groggy from medication. I told him I had bipolar disorder, and I take medication for it. He said he had bipolar disorder, too. He also has anxiety, panic attacks, and PTSD from the military. Same as me, although I was never in the military. He was 38 years old. I will be 38 in 9 days. He was first diagnosed in 2006. Same as me. This was just some random, kindhearted stranger from the neighborhood checking on me. So cool of him to do. Just a very nice, weird thing that happened this morning.

57 ENTRY 57

Having a positive attitude doesn't mean I'm happy all the time. I get in bad moods. Some (parts) of my days are bad sometimes. Mental illness and depression are very real and powerful, but if you start out deciding you are going to have a positive attitude, it's hard to say that you are a failure. I get enjoyment out of making people laugh and smile. I am also very candid about my struggles and illness. At the end of the day, when I'm laying in bed at night, I look back on the day. If I can look back on the day and see that someone was happier or inspired because of my life, I won that day. It's a daily measuring stick that I use to decide if I was successful for the day. I may not have had a great day, but if someone else did because of me, everything I go through is worth it. I am winning at life, despite everything. This is just simply my philosophy of life. It's not something that can be measured. It's not logical like mathematics. I'm just telling you what helps me get through hard days. I know it works because I feel it and live it.

I think most people know that bipolar disorder is a disease of extremes, especially moods. I am somewhat stable most of the time. I don't like it. I like being manic, but it's not good for me. I think I'm so addicted to coffee because it makes me manic sometimes, even at my anxiety's expense. Conversely, I can be in a good mood one minute, and the next minute, it feels like someone punched me in the gut with depression. It's strange and fascinating. I try my best to describe it.

58 ENTRY 58

Here's another poem and commentary I found from 20 years ago, when I was a senior at Moeller High School. Some of these old writings of mine are really weird because you can almost see and feel my mental problems coming on. This was written in the year 2000. I wasn't officially diagnosed until 2006. I guess it just feels weird to me because I wrote it and I remember vaguely how I felt. Like I said before, I'm still the same guy, and maybe my life turned out exactly how it was supposed to. I just took a few detours.

Detached Observer

Don't want to ruin the mood,
I'd never think to intrude,
Upon such important matters dear to you.
I care about everyone else because of all I have felt,
I will emerge in the end,

To see the vision of mirth again.
Dissipate the groups I've come familiar with,
Take away the sanity, which fades to a myth.
Move me along the world with no trace of a journey,
For no trace for anyone to find myself.

COMMENTARY

This poem I wrote when I started to feel that my life was becoming too hectic and rapid for my own mind. I felt that I would be lost in the shuffle of adulthood, and everything is going to change now that I'm entering the real world. I guess I'm scared, but more anxious. I wasn't a very happy person when I wrote this because I feel the pain of other people, and I'm oversensitive to negative occurring in life. I think the world is coming down on me sometimes, and I wonder why I'm here. I think that I may have a mission on this Earth to just simply be funny and nice to others, and I think that's an important vocation. It seems rather simple, but I think I can help others a great deal in the field of psychology to help those who have struggled like myself.

59 ENTRY 59

Do you think that others naturally grow apart as everyone gets older? I always wonder if it's because of my illness that I have lost so many friends and acquaintances. I don't want to believe that my former friends forgot about me on purpose or for any other reason than everyone is busy and has families now and such. When I go out, which is hardly ever, I'm trying really hard to keep the conversation about my books and my illness to a minimum. I care less about being liked, and more about being too much for people or having the conversation get too heavy when people just want to have fun. I also need a break. I have to deal with my illness almost every second, and then I'm advocating on top of that. I don't want my illness and work to define me. I have a lot of substance to my personality.

60 ENTRY 60

I REMEMBER SITTING IN THE EMERGENCY WAITING ROOM. I WAS reading Bible verses to an older black woman. She didn't seem to mind. She was friendly. I remember that much. I went to use the bathroom, and my urine was bright orange, like orange soda. I'm pretty sure I was hallucinating. The doctors took me back into the treatment part of the building. I couldn't calm down. A doctor asked me a bunch of questions—if I knew who the president was and if I was on drugs. She asked me all the drugs I have done, and I had to answer with embarrassment in front of my parents. The nurses gave me a big shot of medicine in my right arm. Shortly after, I laid down in a bed in a room off to the side and slept peacefully for many hours.

61 ENTRY 61

And everything was about politics and war
And now it's always more
Until everything had been bought from every store.
No one wants to leave home
Safety in their gadgets
All the information in the world,
And no one uses it.
Where do we go now?
What's it all for?
Nothing is much use if you don't
Venture from your doors.
To explore everything that has always been there
Just waiting to be enjoyed
But people would rather argue and play with their toys.

JOHN MEDL

62 ENTRY 62

I KNOW I'M A STRONG PERSON, BUT I GUESS I DOUBT HOW STRONG I am going about this whole driving anxiety problem. There's a lot of moments in my life when I say to myself, "Wow. That took a lot of strength". = You are a strong person. I guess I just wonder if I'm being too cautious about driving. When I have physical symptoms of anxiety and panic—chest pains, dizziness, numbness in limbsI feel like I am a danger on the road. Not to mention these symptoms make it extremely difficult to drive.

63 ENTRY 63

I AM MANY THINGS. I'M A SON, BROTHER, AND UNCLE. I'M A ST. Saviour Golden Bear, a Moeller Crusader, and a Dayton Flyer. I'm a good person and a good friend. Some days I feel like I have the magic in me, and some days I feel like I'm just fighting to survive. One thing I am not is a quitter, and no one can take that away from me.

64 ENTRY 64

My maternal grandmother passed away around 1998-1999. Within days of her passing, I started to self medicate with drugs and alcohol. I never thought I'd be a party person like that. I think I was looking for emotional pain relief. I was hurt badly to a point that I had rarely experienced, if ever. In 2006, I was first hospitalized and diagnosed with bipolar disorder. She was a wonderful person. I've never met anyone so devoted to God. If there's anything after this life, I like to think she's looking down on us all, and that I've made her proud. We have a lamp that flickers from old wiring, and my mom says it's my grandma saying hello. It just happened, so I thought I'd write something about her. She never drove a car, and loved getting her hair done. She liked a little wine, and she was a smoker, except for the last few years of her life. I guess it hurt so badly because I thought she'd always be there because she had always been there. I know this sounds like a sad post, but I'm actually reminiscing about her fondly before sleep.

A big problem I have is with confidence. In almost every sense of the word. With my mom breaking her wrist, I've had to do housework that she can't do. I don't know if I thought I couldn't take care of myself or what, but I'm learning that I can should I ever move out on my own. My mom has devoted most of her life to taking care of my dad and my siblings. With me doing some of the housework, it's a good reminder of how much my mom has done for all of us. I cooked dinner tonight for the most part. Laundry. Garbage. I don't take it for granted how much my mom does.

65 ENTRY 65

A BIG PROBLEM I HAVE IS WITH CONFIDENCE. IN ALMOST EVERY sense of the word. With my mom breaking her wrist, I've had to do housework that she can't do. I don't know if I thought I couldn't take care of myself or what, but I'm learning that I can should I ever move out on my own. My mom has devoted most of her life to taking care of my dad and my siblings. With me doing some of the housework, it's a good reminder of how much my mom has done for all of us. I cooked dinner tonight for the most part. Laundry. Garbage. I don't take it for granted how much my mom does.

66 ENTRY 66

I SEE STUFF ALL THE TIME ON SOCIAL MEDIA AND WHEREVER ELSE that talk about people on disability or public assistance. It's almost always negative and judgemental. Yes, some people abuse the system and fake disability, but I don't believe that's usually the case. But guess what? It's not anyone's business. Yes, tax dollars pay for public assistance, but what about the people who become disabled who paid into Social Security for years? God forbid anything happens to you or your family where you need public assistance. Mr. or Mrs. Jones is allowed to have nice things even if they are food stamps. Maybe they bought their nice items before they became disabled. Maybe they have a rich uncle or something. You just never know. That's why being judgemental makes people look ignorant. Personally, it took me 7 years to get approved for disability. The whole process was ridiculous and nearly impossible. I had a lawyer, but I dumped every one finally, and I was losing hope. The way I got approved was my mother took all my records with a picture of me to the Social Security/Disability office, and shortly after, I was approved. It was a miracle for my family. I don't know where all these people are who are rich off the government, but it's not me. I would kill to be able to work a normal job. I would make a hell of a lot more money. My parents taught me the values of hard work, so I try to do what I can to feel like I am earning those disability payments and $38 a month in food assistance. I know not everyone is like that, but that's me. I don't worry about everyone else.

67 ENTRY 67

During this pandemic, I see people being kinder to each other, in general of course. I see people respecting the elderly again. I see musicians finding new ways to perform. I see people making art and enjoying the outdoors. I see parents cherishing lost time with their kids. Maybe we needed a break and the world to stop for a minute...(obviously I know all of this has come at a great cost to a lot of people)

68 ENTRY 68

I'VE BEEN DEPRESSED FOR A FEW WEEKS OFF AND ON. IT'S ALWAYS off and on because of the duality of bipolar disorder. I've thought about what I might say if I knew it was the last of my time on Earth. I've thought about what my eulogy might sound like. Thoughts about death and dying are common with anxiety, depression, and bipolar disorder. There's as high as a 20% suicide rate for bipolar disorder as well. If I ever get to that point, I have faith that I would tell someone. Or write about it as I'm doing now. I've thought about my parents aging, and the real possibility that they might not be around some day. As always, the reason I'm writing this is for the greater good. You are not alone. If my symptoms aren't too bad, you can talk to me. Please get help if you need it or find an outlet that gives you relief.

69 ENTRY 69

From a reader:

Dear Mr. Medl,

I am a freshman student at the University of Vermont, enrolled in a class to discuss mental health disorders.

I have just read your book Millions Like Me, so I know reading is difficult for you.

Perhaps you have someone to help you read, but if not, I will try to keep this email short and space it so hopefully, it's easier.

I just wanted to say thank you for your book.

I do not currently think I have any mental disorders (I just turned 18) but this book was incredibly helpful and insightful for me regardless.

I of course cannot begin to imagine the work you put into writing it, but it's so valuable to learn from.

Your poems, while tinted with sadness and isolation, are truly powerful and beautiful to read.

Again, thank you

70 ENTRY 70

There's nothing for me on the other side
And I'm fine with that
Even if it is just an eternal dirt nap
What if there's more?
I'm tired and sore
I'm tired of thinking
My thoughts have always been my enemy
I just want to live silently
Head down.
Put in my days.
I just want to feel the sun's rays.
But the rain has its place.
You might even see a smile on my face
I want to feel content enough to be kind
My mind has failed me
But I trust my heart
Even when I fell apart

71 ENTRY 71

I'VE BEEN DEPRESSED FOR A FEW WEEKS OFF AND ON. IT'S ALWAYS off and on because of the duality of bipolar disorder. I've thought about what I might say if I knew it was the last of my time on Earth. I've thought about what my eulogy might sound like. Thoughts about death and dying are common with anxiety, depression, and bipolar disorder. There's as high as a 20% suicide rate for bipolar disorder as well. If I ever get to that point, I have faith that I would tell someone. Or write about it as I'm doing now. I've thought about my parents aging, and the real possibility that they might not be around some day. As always, the reason I'm writing this is for the greater good. You are not alone. If my symptoms aren't too bad, you can talk to me. Please get help if you need it or find an outlet that gives you relief.

72 ENTRY 72

Going through psychosis and being delusional is a strange thing, especially when I snapped out of it and back to another reality. I remember a lot of the insane things I thought and acted upon, and it just hurts. I think because it's so embarrassing. Not to mention how painful it was to go through that trauma. People I've known for a very long time witnessed my insanity, and like I said, it's so embarrassing. I'm sure when some people think of me, they think of the insane things I did, and not the actual person who I really am. I am not my illness. I've had a lot of great times in my life, and it seems like good times are rare for me anymore. I get in moods where I get so agitated that not even my mother's voice is comforting. I think about how nice eternal silence is going to be. I don't really believe in complaining, but I still experience a lot of pain—physical, mental, and emotional. Some days, I think I'm ready to call it quits, or if my life ended, I would be fine with it. I've paid back society and done my time. This is what bipolar depression looks and sounds like. I'm lost as to what helps or what can help me bring me out of a funk like this. I can't even think straight except for negative and depressing thoughts. I hold on to the hopes that it will pass as it always does. It helps when I joke around and make people laugh, or when I feel like I really reached someone who is also struggling. I felt like I didn't really know what to do right now, so I wrote it down, and I feel a little better. I'm going to try to practice some self-care tonight and just take it easy. Find something relaxing to do. I haven't read a single page of any book in a while, and I have a lot of interesting books I want to read. Self care might mean taking a shower or watching something mindless on TV. I wish I could figure it out like a math problem, but depression is rarely logical.

73 ENTRY 73

I WAS SUPPOSED TO HAVE A PHONE CALL MEETING/ASSESSMENT with my psychiatrist today, but he was out of the office. I was looking forward to it because I wanted to talk about some emotional issues I've been having lately. I got rescheduled for 10 days from now, so it's all good. As much as I've written, I don't think I've ever just flat out said that mental illness is really hard to deal with. Maybe a few times, but not often. I don't like talking about it, and I hate complaining and excuses. Mental illness and not having a properly functioning brain has BY FAR been the hardest thing I've ever had to deal with. The worst day of my life was when I was first hospitalized in 2006. Although I wasn't completely coherent, but I remember more than I should. I've tried to make the most of my situation and stay positive by writing and cracking jokes, etc., but it's really hard on me sometimes. I know a lot of you out there have to deal with all sorts of things that maybe you don't talk about.

No matter what the ailment, you are not alone. I struggle a lot too. Like I said, I do a pretty good job of playing it off, but my mental illness can be unforgiving.

74 ENTRY 74

I HAD A MEETING OVER THE PHONE WITH MY PSYCHIATRIST TODAY. He's very positive. He reminded me of how far I have come and told me I am doing a good job. If I could only internalize what others see in me. I am an overthinker and my own biggest critic and enemy. Even after all this time, I am still a work in progress. I don't know if I will ever be satisfied. My doctor even said that he wishes he could put me on payroll to talk to some of his other clients. I have been completely compliant, especially with medication, which is not my nature at all. I put my trust in the experts' hands, and they delivered. Before my diagnosis, I never even took Advil or Tylenol, much less psychotropic medications. Somewhere deep down, I know I am a success story. I know I inspire people. I know I am blessed, and I am grateful for everything I have and everything I've worked for. I have a sick brain that tells me lies and sometimes I can't convince myself that I'm actually doing pretty well compared to my mental health history. I guess it was nice to hear from my doctor. I've been humbled to the point of rock bottom, but I still believe there is something special about me. I've emptied the tank, so to speak, for so long and so many days trying to fight this illness. It's exhausting and frustrating, but I've never quit, which is something to hang my hat on. When I try to sleep at night, I remind myself that I am doing the best I can to provide some sort of mental comfort.

75 ENTRY 75

I CONQUERED ONE OF MY BIGGEST AND LONGEST LINGERING FEARS today. I saw a primary care doctor and had blood drawn. It had been about 10 years since both events. Everyone who gave me medical attention was great. My blood pressure was a little high, but not concerning. The blood work is the standard tests —kidney and liver functions, sugars, and metabolism. I guess you can't just be fat anymore haha. I have faith and hope in humanity, even if it is only temporary. What matters to me more is having faith and confidence in myself. It's a lot easier for me to help humanity when I feel good about myself. I can't help anyone if I don't believe in my abilities. I don't need faith in humanity. I've seen what it is—good and evil, ups and downs, lies and truth. It's always going to be that way. I just try to do my part, and I can't do that to my fullest ability without confidence, faith, and trust in myself.

76 ENTRY 76

There's noise coming from the magic box
As I roll up another cigarette
The actors have rehearsed their lines
Handed down to them by people
Who have never had to fight for anything
The brave warriors slave away
For a hundred dollars a day
If they're lucky
So the privileged can live in decadence
It's been this way for such a long time
When will this change like society has?
Fear and masks
All we know how to do is pray
I wonder if anyone is listening

77 ENTRY 77

Mania is a hallmark feature of bipolar disorder. When manic, a person can impulsively spend money or have trouble budgeting money. I have experienced this many times, and it's something I struggle with. Today, I was able to open my own checking account. For years, I have been sharing an account with my mom, and it has caused a lot of stress in my family. Glad to check another thing off the list, working towards more independence and responsibility.

78 ENTRY 78

One of the hardest lessons I'm still trying to learn is that not everyone is going to like me. There's a saying that goes, "You could be the ripest, juiciest peach in the world, and there's still going to be people who don't like peaches". Honestly, it's their loss. I'm loyal to a fault, and I have a lot to offer, I would never screw anyone over intentionally, and I don't wish harm on anyone, not even the people who have done me wrong.

79 ENTRY 79

Sometimes, I think to myself, "Why does anyone care what I write about?", but then I think, "Why does anyone care what anyone writes about? Why not me?" I'm not some expert who is just writing about something I've read in books. I've lived the Hell that I write about. I think that's one of many reasons why people gravitate towards me and are interested in reading my books. If you read my books, you will find that I am brutally honest about my symptoms and my experiences. Just something to think about for any aspiring writers. I also hope that my honestly does not come off as complaining because sometimes I think there's nothing worse. It's a toxic trait that creates a negative environment. I try to be grateful and humble. It's a challenge. It's much harder to be grateful and courageous in the face of adversity than the alternative.

80 ENTRY 80

Yesterday, I had a meeting with my clinical diagnostician, and today with my case manager. Relatively painless stuff. We basically laid out a treatment plan for the year. I wish I didn't have to do stuff like this, but it's probably for my own good. I really just want to be free and left alone most of the time, but all my meetings are good reminders of my goals and progress I suppose.

81 ENTRY 81

My parents are sleeping, so y'all are going to have to deal with my rantings. Before I wrote this, the office chair broke, which is supposed to have an 800 pound capacity or something. This is like the third one that has broken on me. I'm not slim, but I'm not 800 pounds.

We had to have a new sump pump installed in the basement today, which is basically not my territory of business, but it's just something that happened today.

The Department of Education forgave the remaining balance of my student loans years ago, but they still send mail to check up on me to make sure I haven't become wealthy or gainfully employed. Not a huge deal, but stressful and annoying in some small way.

Here's the really annoying thing. I started a checking account with $40 a few weeks ago, and it was overdrawn this morning. Every time I made a transaction, I checked the banking app first to make sure the money was there. When I set up the account, I told the people to make sure that no purchases would be approved if the money wasn't there. When I went to bed last night, I had about a dollar in my account, which is fine because when I set up the account, I made sure there was no minimum balance requirement. I MADE SURE all of these things to safeguard against an over-withdrawal. When I woke up this morning, I had to deal with the stress of my account being way overdrawn, and not just by a little. No one at the bank wanted to take responsibility, and everyone around me just assumed it was my fault because I've had a few bouts of financial irresponsibility. I guess it's at least partially my fault because I was the one at the controls, but I was so careful. I was even keeping track with pen and paper because I felt like something wasn't right. Long story short, fuck today. Let's hope for a better tomorrow.

82 ENTRY 82

Panic attacks are shocking in a lot of ways. I'm not sure if that's the right word. I'm just always shocked at how painful they are and that I've survived so many. I just had a brief panic attack, and they are not for the weak. My entire body gets stiff, and my mind races in nonsensical words and phrases. I get dizzy and I get stomach cramps. I just took an Advil to try to kill some of the physical pain. Loud noises are almost unbearable to tolerate, but soft and familiar music sometimes helps me. I roll cigarettes to try to distract myself. I try to move around to make the body stiffness better. When my stomach settles, I'm going to eat dinner and rest. That's how I deal with them. It's over after that. Then the battle begins again. This doesn't happen to me often, and I've actually been making some good progress.

83 ENTRY 83

Some victories that I've had lately:

1. I opened my own checking account so that I could be financially independent
2. Some of my family members visited for dinner, so I got to see them. I had anxiety almost the whole time, but I got through it.
3. I successfully completed 3 meetings this week--- one with my clinical diagnostician, one with my case manager, and one with my psychiatrist. We laid out a treatment plan for the next year, and my medications are staying the same, but that may change. My doctor didn't want to change anything because he hasn't seen me in person for months. I've been on the same medication for about 8 years now.
4. I filled out some official paperwork regarding the forgiveness of my student loans

5. I drove myself to the store and to the bank. I have major driving anxiety, and sometimes I can't drive at all.

All of these things are hard for me. They are challenges, and considered victories when I complete them. I think I had too many things going on in one week, so that's probably why I have had increased anxiety and panic attacks.

84 ENTRY 84

Whenever I have a visit with my psychiatrist, he always asks the same beginning questions...."Do you think you can fly or do you think you have superpowers?" and "Are you hearing voices?". These may seem like strange questions to the average person, but I have answered "yes" to these questions before. Quick example. When I was first hospitalized in 2006, I was convinced that I could jump off the balcony at the hospital and "fly" or land safely below. I have no idea what stopped me. I have a "loud brain", which basically means I have an active inner dialogue. Not everyone has that, so I've found out. It serves me well with writing, but it's extremely annoying and exhausting when I'm trying to rest. As long as the "voices" aren't directive (telling me to do a specific thing), then I'm considered stable enough, I guess. I've had problems with directive voices/psychosis before also. I can only explain psychosis as watching myself in a movie and someone or something else is at the controls. I've always had a loud brain, but I haven't had problems with psychosis or extreme grandeur in a long time.

Am I angry at life because of my mental illness? Not usually. I don't see how that's productive, and the world doesn't owe me anything. It could always be worse. Even when I don't have any money, I'm richer than a lot of people across the world. I wish I were a stronger person so that I acted as blessed as I feel, but I'm just human with limitations. I've tried not to use my illness as a crutch, but it is a good explanation for a lot of my behavior. For me, mental illness is frustrating, painful, and exhausting. I've prayed for death and thought about taking my own life. My best days are when I get some relief. It doesn't happen often, as my illness is mostly relentless. I've chosen to educate others through my books and volunteer my time to help others find some relief. So many positive things have come from my illness, and it helps me to focus on all the good things rather than feel sorry for myself.

85 ENTRY 85

June 9, 2020—In the middle of a global pandemic and racial protests

I don't feel guilty for being white. I didn't get to choose my skin color as much as anyone. But I do understand what white privilege means. As a white person, I'm more likely to have access to all kinds of resources and less likely to be harassed by the police. It doesn't mean that my life is easy. I know good cops. I've known them almost my whole life. But once you are mistreated by the police, how do you forget that? My former professor is Latino and he was brutalized and beaten by police in Minnesota. He won a lawsuit against them. I'm seeing a lot of positive changes in the form of diversity programs and funding for minority causes. It's very strange as a white person. I think I was so used to everyday racism that I was comfortable. Change is usually uncomfortable, and I want to be part of the solution, and I want to be on the right side of history. If racial equality is going to happen, white people need to help because we're still running the show.

86 ENTRY 86

I HAD A PRETTY GOOD DAY TODAY:

1. I took a shower. Embarrassingly, it had been a while
2. I balanced my checking account, and the balance is positive.
3. I drove myself to the doctor for a sore jaw. He prescribed me antibiotics for the infection. I'll probably have to see a dentist, barring some miracle, but still a victory for me.

87 ENTRY 87

I'VE GOT TO LEARN TO NOT BE SO HARD ON MYSELF

I'm a lucky, blessed man. Everyone is so kind to me, especially my mom, the rest of my family, and close friends. I know this sounds stupid, but I feel like if I remind myself of my blessings even in hard times, that I will somehow heal faster. In a way, it does help me heal faster. Reminding myself of my good fortune at the very least occupies my mind with positive thoughts. I'm a simple man. I don't need much to be happy.

88 ENTRY 88

Mania is often referred to as a "high", like a drug. It's like the highest you've ever been off drugs that are in your brain. No street drugs compare. That's how intense it is. I've heard, "Medication took my superpowers away." That high. Delusional and psychotic high.

89 ENTRY 89

I'VE HAD PROBABLY THOUSANDS OF PANIC ATTACKS, BUT I remember this one in particular. I remember smoking 9 cigarettes in a row. I just couldn't calm down. It goes that way sometimes. I remember because I counted. It's an OCD thing. I also roll my cigarettes in even numbers because I smoke 2 in a row while I'm out on the porch. I will always contend that mental illness is the hardest thing I've ever had to endure. Every day I survive is a notch in my belt. I'm extremely proud of myself for never giving up.

90 ENTRY 90

I should have known something was wrong in college, but then again, I showed symptoms in high school and childhood. We all just had no idea. In college, I engaged in risky behavior, but I had this delusion that lights turned off when I was around. Like street lamps. It seemed like it happened a lot. Then, I told my friends, and they noticed too, which reinforced my delusion. The logical explanation is that these lights were on timers, and it was coincidental that the lights would turn off. I thought it was some kind of supernatural thing, but I didn't take it very seriously and kind of brushed it off.

91 ENTRY 91

One of my best friends visited the other day. He's known me since high school. He visited me in the hospital and has bought all my books. I try not to talk about my illness in regular conversation, but it always seems to come up. It occurred to me that I never really asked about this friend's mental health.

So I simply asked, "Do you have depression or anxiety or anything?"

And he simply said, "No".

It kind of blew my mind because I thought about how nice it would be to not have anxiety or depression, but I do remember a long time ago when I didn't have to worry about my mental health. It's an incredible blessing to not have to deal with. However, my buddy has physical health problems that I don't have to deal with, so his life is far from being a walk in the park.

92 ENTRY 92

On July 31, 2020, I will celebrate being a 14 year survivor of mental illness from the first time I was hospitalized. Mental illness tried to take my life many times, but my spirit was not having any of it. I really hope I get a chance to talk to the students of Moeller HS about mental health. When I attended Moeller, there wasn't much talk about mental health. All the advocacy work I do makes me feel like I'm fulfilling my purpose. That somehow, some way, makes me feel I am exactly where I am supposed to be, and I'm doing exactly what I am supposed to be doing. It's a great feeling to feel like you are fulfilling your purpose in life. The fear of dying with unfinished business goes away. The age old question of "Have I done enough with my life?" goes away. Whatever I have sacrificed for stability (most of the time), I have gained in perspective and purpose. I am extremely grateful for my life and how it turned out. I wasn't always so optimistic. I had to work at it. I've lost plenty of battles, but I feel like I am winning the war. That's as close to beating mental illness as you can get, in my opinion.

I just want to talk about intelligence for a minute because it's on my mind. I am going to describe my family because there are 7 of us (my parents and 5 siblings) because I think it is a good example of the varieties of intelligence. You don't need a college degree to be smart, but I think it helps. I also know people who didn't graduate high school who are master musicians and carpenters.

I guess I will start with my dad. My dad has a two-year degree from The University of Cincinnati. He is an electrical engineer by trade. He must be good with money too because we don't have a whole lot of it, but we rarely go without necessities. My mom didn't finish college. It wasn't really a popular thing for women to do in the 1960s. However, she has raised 5 kids with good values and morals with not too many injuries haha. She is an extremely hard worker, which I think is a type of intelligence in a way. She is also very organized, which I think is another kind of intelligence. My oldest brother is a radar specialist for a government contractor out in Arizona. He has a Master's Degree. My next brother never finished college, but he is a master carpenter and very good at investing and money. My sister never finished college, but she is an office manager who oversees collecting invoices for a billboard company. My closest brother has a Master's Degree in Mathematics and is extremely book smart and computer smart. He's the brother we call when our computer screws up. Then there's me, the youngest of all of us. I consider myself intelligent, but like everyone else, I have my moments of dim bulbness. I just wanted to write about my family because I love them all, of course, but I think we are all intelligent in our own way. Some of us have degrees, and some don't. It doesn't have to be an either/or thing where you are smart if you have a degree, and dumb if you do not. All of this probably just relates to the fact that you shouldn't judge people, and it seems like it comes down to that a lot.

93 ENTRY 93

My spending was out of control this month, so I gave control of my finances to my brother. My checking account is closed, credit cards are frozen, and I don't have any way to move money with apps like Venmo and PayPal. I'm a little disappointed in myself, but I know it's for the best. I was borrowing money from a lot of people, mainly to gamble, and it had to stop to get this household's finances in order, and also to plan for the future. Gambling gave me hope that I could win a lot of money in a short time because I can't work a standard job. The writing job I was hoping for isn't going to work out either. On the bright side, I drove myself to the store, and I'm getting closer to finishing my fourth book each day. I'm just having a difficult time.

94 ENTRY 94

So here's a story that I've never told before. Damn, I remember it like it was yesterday. It was at least 10 years ago at Good Samaritan Hospital. I was being treated for psychosis and panic. One of the nurses gave me a pill and asked me how I felt. "Heavenly", I said. I was looking out into the sun-setting sky, and that's really how I felt. Several times. I've felt a supernatural force acting upon me, usually good, but sometimes evil feeling. I found out later that the pill was just for heartburn, but I think I answered in that way because that's what I thought the nurses wanted me to say. I'm not really sure. I do vaguely remember actually feeling that supernatural, heavenly way. I don't think anyone can truly understand psychosis and mania unless you have been through it. I don't care how many degrees you have. You have to feel it and experience it. Some people describe mania as a high, but that doesn't fully encompass the feeling. It's not like a let's smoke a blunt in high school high. It's like the best drug you have ever taken, combined with the worst hallucinogenic drug you have ever taken times a million. And psychosis is like watching yourself in a movie, with someone else at the controls.

95 ENTRY 95

When I was 618 pounds, I should have just hung it up and let nature take its course. I didn't. I don't use a scale, but I'm almost certain that I've lost over 100 pounds. Every time I was hospitalized, people would have understood if I quit. When I had to take medication, that made me feel absolutely awful, I should have given up. When I was lying on the couch in a medicinal haze, I should have just stayed down. I kept getting up and forcing myself to take showers when it felt impossible. When I had panic attacks while driving, people would have understood if I quit trying to drive. I wasn't raised that way. We (my siblings) weren't taught to quit. We were taught to fight. Our parents led by example in many ways, but the most impressive was that my mom and dad each beat cancer twice. My dad only has one kidney. In all honesty, I don't know how I survived a lot of things I have. I don't know why I didn't quit when I didn't know what I was doing. My mind was gone, and I still didn't quit. Now, I'm about to be an author for the fourth time. I'm going to be mentioned in the Fall Newsletter for my alma mater, Moeller High School. I'm also trying to get a mention from my college alma mater, The University of Dayton, but they have been unresponsive to my messages. I've worked with the Cincinnati-based non-profit 1N5.org on several projects. I'm the founder and administrator of a social media page devoted to mental illness and inspiration for 8 years now. We have almost 800 members. At times, I don't know how I've come this far, but I'm glad I did. Yes, I'm bragging about myself. I've earned it.

96 ENTRY 96

Well, today's the day. I survived another year. Fourteen years ago today (July 31, 2006), my life fell apart. I lost my house, car, job, girlfriend, and any reputation I had as a sane person. I was rushed to the hospital with what they call a psychotic first break of bipolar disorder. I stayed in a locked down psychiatric unit for 11 days. It was a nightmare, and I still have flashbacks sometimes, even after all these years. I am extremely proud of how I have handled all my diagnoses and what I have accomplished. I have made my family and friends proud. I have a grateful and loving heart. I appreciate life now more than I ever did before. I tell everyone that I am blessed. I have everything I need, which is more than a lot of people have. At some point in my recovery, I decided I wanted to do more than just survive and exist. I've made lemonade, as they say, and I've played the cards I have been dealt to the best of my abilities. I can't express enough my gratitude for all the support in every capacity. The love that has been shown to me, by all sorts of people, has been tremendous. I am just a humble servant trying to carry out a mission of kindness and awareness of mental health issues. Thank you for your support. For being there for me. It absolutely makes a difference.

97 ENTRY 97

I don't want to be young again, but if I could go back in time for a weekend in high school, I think I would agree to that. Party all weekend without a care or responsibility. Barely sleep, except on Sunday to recover for the upcoming week of classes. No smart phones or every app imaginable. Not many people had cell phones, either. I can't remember if I did or not. I remember people having pagers, which I never had. No Netflix and the like or social media. We took pictures with disposable cameras and actually had to wait to get the pictures developed. Weekend long binges at music festivals with a bunch of mostly kindhearted strangers just camping and listening to music. I think of those days fondly, but I still would only want to go back for a weekend. I enjoy my life now as a writer and mental health advocate. I appreciate peace of mind and silence. I don't like party atmospheres anymore. I don't think I'm boring. I just lived the party lifestyle already, and I'm done with it all. I want to keep those fond memories just as memories, and thank my lucky stars that I survived. Now, at age 38, I feel like I don't know about so many things, and I was so confident, borderline cocky in high school, which is amazing, because I was incredibly stupid compared to now. But I would still go back for a weekend if I had the chance. Maybe I am just feeling nostalgic today.

98 ENTRY 98

I used to believe in the good in everyone. The world has shown me that's not true. I used to think that bad people were just good people who did bad and evil things. I think people either chose to be evil or they are born that way, or some combination. That's usually how it goes in psychology. Nothing is really ever black and white. On a psychology exam, the answer is rarely straightforward. The answer is usually all of the above, none of the above, or both A and C. Things like that. I studied out of a philosophy book that was titled, "Taking Sides", and if I remember correctly, it was all about how people don't have to always take a side on every topic. You can agree or disagree with some parts of one side or the other. I think people get trapped into thinking in black and white terms, so when they are confronted with conflicting evidence of their beliefs, they won't give an inch because they have chosen a side. It's very hard for people to change their minds once they are made up. I believe this is the spirit of cognitive dissonance.

I remember writing a whole term paper on rationalization. It was either a psychology or philosophy course. In many ways, those two subjects overlap and are related. Anyway, the thesis of my paper is that rationalization is extremely dangerous because you can rationalize almost anything. Right now, I am fighting a gambling addiction. I have been gambling half of my life. It turned from recreational to a maniacal addiction. I don't like to use bipolar disorder as an excuse, but it definitely is an explanation and played a role. I was so stressed out about my parents' finances and their health. Every time I gambled, I thought I was going to win. It's really hard to give up because I have won a lot of money gambling. It was getting to the point where I was borrowing money and losing control. It had to stop. Maybe one day, I can recreationally gamble again, but for now, I am sickened by the idea, and I am trying to find myself again and finish this book. Getting back to my point, I rationalized my gambling habit because I don't drink alcohol or do drugs. I thought my gambling was acceptable because I didn't have those other coping mechanisms that most people have. You can rationalize anything if you lie to yourself enough.

99 ENTRY 99

I don't even know where to start. Last night, I was extremely depressed. I was watching a poker tournament on my phone, and I was just thinking about how nice it would be to have the money to play. I've been in a poker club for about 10 years now, and the tournament entrants were my friends. We usually play in person, but because of the pandemic virus, everyone plays on an online computer application. I haven't been able to play in person for several years now, with the exception of one night, because it's hard for me to concentrate that long and sit still. The key to live poker is to be as unreadable (a la poker faced) as possible, and my anxiety gives me away every time. It's not even fun anymore.

My checking account is closed. All my credit cards are cut up and my credit is frozen. I have no access to any gambling sites on the computer. I have no access to money applications on my phone to move money around. All of this is for the betterment of myself and my situation, as well as lightening the worry and burden on my parents and siblings. I know that. I'm trying to accept that. I don't know if I need a night out with my friends or if I need someone to visit me, or what. Sometimes I just feel like running away and starting a new life. I think about living in a tiny place with few possessions by a body of water and just living there until I die without talking to anyone again. I feel stuck. I don't know if I should live here with my parents or go start a new life somewhere. I don't even know if I could handle living on my own or afford it for that matter. I don't want to abandon everyone, but I really do get that urge a lot. Maybe I'm just tired or anxious or otherwise symptomatic right now. I could barely sit still enough to write this entry.

Journaling is a coping mechanism for me, but it's also a force where I feel compelled to write like my brain needs to throw up, per se. Writing helps release the pressure in my mind of all my thoughts. I wonder if other writers or artists or musicians feel that creative force too.

I don't know if it's possible for the living to understand suicide, but I feel like I do. A long time ago, I was suicidal, but I never attempted it. I've had suicidal thoughts too. Mental illness and anguish is incredible pain, and my best guess is that it gets to be too great for some people. I don't think people who commit or attempt suicide are cowards. I think they're just humans who have had too much pain to bear. My writing and mental health advocacy have given me purpose, which helps me when my thoughts get dark. I don't really have suicidal thoughts anymore. I've had to call my case manager several times because I was in mental anguish, and I'm always confident that I will ask for help if I need it. I know the world is a better place with me in it. I know my family and friends would be sad, and I want to go down swinging with dignity. Even with all these great reasons to live, the dark thoughts still creep in sometimes. Mental illness is incredible pain, as I mentioned. Most of the time, I feel okay. I feel good about my life and my contribution to society. But the small amount of time when I am symptomatic is incredibly painful.

It is currently August of the year 2020. I live in Cincinnati, Ohio. There's a global pandemic ravaging through the world with staggering infection rates and fatalities. I don't know if life will ever be the same again. I'm hoping and praying that the pandemic eventually subsides, and a sense of normalcy returns.

100 ENTRY 100

THIS BOOK IS RANDOM IN A LOT OF WAYS, BUT I WANTED IT TO BE that way. Mental illness can be very fluid and different every day. I think the goal of any treatment and medication regimen is stability, but it doesn't always work that way. I can have a span of a month where every day is a different battle, but I can also have a span of a month or several that are stable and much easier to contend with. I can't tell you exactly when I wrote all of the entries in this book, but I think it represents the volatility of my illness and mental illness in general. When I decided to become a writer and mental health advocate, my main goal was to bring awareness to mental health issues and to make others feel like they are not alone. I hope I have done that in this book and all my books. Much love to you all.

ALSO BY JOHN MEDL

Millions Like Me: My Struggle with Mental Illness: books2read.com/Millions-Like-Me

Poems From a Bipolar Mind: books2read.com/Poems-Bipolar

The Last Day of July: 13 Years of Madness: books2read.com/Last-Day-July

The Entropy of Bipolar Disorder: books2read.com/Entropy-Bipolar

Mental Illness Is An Actual Illness: books2read.com/Mental-Illness-Actual-Illness

Making Bipolar Lemonade: books2read.com/Bipolar-Lemonade

Bipolar Rising : books2read.com/Bipolar-Rising

ABOUT JOHN MEDL

John Medl is an author with over five published books and a mental health advocate from Cincinnati, Ohio. He has suffered from mental illness for more than eleven years. His diagnoses are: bipolar disorder with psychotic features, obsessive-compulsive disorder, Post-Traumatic Stress Disorder, Generalized Anxiety-Panic Disorder, claustrophobia, and agoraphobia.

John has a Bachelor of Arts in Psychology from the University of Dayton, which he finds ironic.

books2read.com/John-Medl

facebook.com/john.medl

twitter.com/johnmedl7

instagram.com/johnmedl7

amazon.com/author/john-medl

www.ingramcontent.com/pod-product-compliance
Lightning Source LLC
LaVergne TN
LVHW022221200926
848481LV00006B/2061
* 9 7 9 8 2 1 5 5 7 8 3 4 6 *